ONE LITTLE ROOM

Peter McDonald was born in Belfast in 1962. His first book of poetry, *Biting the Wax*, was published in 1989, and since then seven volumes of his verse have appeared, including his *Collected Poems* (2012). He has written four books of literary criticism, including *Mistaken Identities: Poetry and Northern Ireland* (1997) and *Sound Intentions: The Workings of Rhyme in Nineteenth-Century Poetry* (2012), and has edited Louis MacNeice's *Collected Poems* (2007) and most recently three volumes of the Longman *Poems of W.B. Yeats*. He is Emeritus Professor of British and Irish Poetry at Oxford University, and an Emeritus Student of Christ Church, Oxford.

One Little Room
Peter McDonald

CARCANET POETRY

First published in Great Britain in 2024 by
Carcanet
Alliance House, 30 Cross Street
Manchester, M 2   7 A Q
www.carcanet.co.uk

A CIP catalogue record for this book is
available from the British Library.

ISBN 978 1 80017 449 8

Book design by Andrew Latimer, Carcanet
Typesetting by LiteBook Prepress Services
Printed in Great Britain by SRP Ltd, Exeter, Devon

The publisher acknowledges financial
assistance from Arts Council England.

CONTENTS

For Cassy

et la mer au matin comme une présomption de l'esprit.

– St.-John Perse, *Anabase*, I

ONE LITTLE ROOM

THE TRUNK

I was leaving home, now I was crossing the water
to where I would need everything – bedclothes, books,
towels and crockery, a kettle, a toaster –
and all of that was more than could be carried:
the solution was to send it on ahead, and so
Dad took me to Smithfield market to find a trunk.

To what was left of Smithfield: once, it was where
(he said) you could find anything in the world
you needed – though that was a long time ago –
and when we got into town on Saturday,
within ten minutes – *look, that's the very dab* –
we had found and bought and taken away the trunk.

It set out maybe a week ahead of me,
never to return: at first, it was furniture
in a little room, just sturdy enough to sit on,
then it summered in storerooms, went to basements
where it held nothing that was ever much needed,
and five or six years later, I had lost the trunk.

It was small, about four feet, but deep enough
to climb completely inside if you bent double,
with the outside a dull, metal-effect grey,
stickered and stained, and the clasps brass-coloured:
everything it used to hold must have gone for scrap,
and when I last saw it, it was just an empty trunk.

But you never know when something will be needed,
at least, I was told so – advice I ignored –
and maybe now it's exactly that emptiness
I want for what I hold only a last time
then pack away: all of this stuff weighs nothing,
and it could lie safe forever in that trunk.

THE FOUNTAIN IN LADY DIXON PARK

It was a little circle about two feet high,
      a shallow dish
where the slight shapes of a few goldfish
would navigate, and lazily turn by
      the short, thin stick
I stirred the surface with, working around
      one water-lily
on that autumn morning in nineteen sixty-
five, as I tip-toed on the gravelled ground:
      not a fountain really,
no burst of vapour pluming a clear sky,
but at the centre enough of a jump and splash
of drops to keep me listening, as I
      leaned on cold stone
to scan the surface of a round ocean
that was filling itself from that slapdash
spout in the middle; I wasn't alone,
for others my size had all been drawn in,
making a loose circle, never again
      together in one place
(they might be grandparents now, or some dead),
and in this snapshot mine is the one face
I recognize, though barely, laughing on
      under a bobble hat,
through a second not to be repeated
that matters to no one, that doesn't matter,
      and the water-patter
has stopped long since, and that fountain is dry,
or maybe it's filled with soil, and planted
up with low shrubs, as if in memory

of something forgotten that was briefly there –
       spray faint in the air,
and children at play just before a war,
forgotten too, in time as far away
       as shallows where
the frail fish-spirits move, not knowing why.

TEARS

My first proper poem, forty years ago,
had muses in it – the muses were real girls;
real girls were muses: as if it was true,
they were all crying as they walked in circles.

SOLITUDE

Paraphrase on St.-John Perse, Anabase IV

The gannet I found stranded in a car-park,
something all wrong with its wings
and its head too heavy for the neck to bear,
beautiful bird, beautiful ugly bird.

*

Not the street-parties day and night tomorrow,
but the morning after that, and the bin-men
redding up shredded pieces of palm-trees
like the *débris* of enormous wings.

*

The gannet's eyes, the gannet's big clown-face.

*

A touch of yellow, and the town in yellow light,
close, damp, and heavy now with a storm coming;
shadows that latch the streets, and windows open
where dresses flap and hang, and never dry.

*

A great sea-going bird's single blue egg.

MOTHERS

1.

for Elise Paschen

The one and only time I meet your mother
my knowledge of you is a good three-quarters
'On a Plane Flying down the Coast of Florida'
and twenty-something glamour; now here we are
pushing sixty, and talking about her
when she had to cook for Auden or Stravinsky
(or was it Auden and Stravinsky together?)
in a little apartment in New York City
though nearly all of her twenty-three years
had been spent dancing, dancing, dancing
from Fairfax Oklahoma, and the Osage,
to California and Monte Carlo, dancing
against her parents' wishes into marriage
a long time before happiness, and you.
She fiddles about in that tiny kitchen
as the great men talk their talk, and it's taken
all this time for me to know what to do,
to fetch clean knives and forks out of the drawer
then clear a space and stack away the saucepans,
so she can move as gracefully as ever before;
and she dances again now, precisely weaving
through your poems, on points, abolishing gravity
and so balanced there that she can never leave.

2.
for Rosanna Warren

Peering like experts into the oven, we
check on the vegetables and roasting salmon,
till I turn and there on the wall behind me
is the face of the most beautiful young woman
I already knew: she was twenty-one
and orbiting close in to the *Partisan Review*
when he fell – collapsed – in love with her, then
wrote letters where his heart, brimming with ice,
cracked into torrents. And you know all this,
remembering her memories: how she
had liked him well enough, but – as our children
might say – she just wasn't that into him.
The apartment windows are Chicago at night time,
but even this long away, we flinch. You send
me your poem about the snake, that great sum
of small pain we absorb and move on from,
which lessens us, or doesn't, as the case
may be; it's March, and I'm shivering; I see
you both at the end in Judith's photograph,
and imagine her hands clasped cold in yours.
As a girl, she almost died once in the snow,
but now her twenty-odd, encumbered years
leave her to quarrel with the Irish poet
about politics, and how it all matters
apart from love: when he dreams of her, she
is a skater, and she has another name,
dancing across the lake when the lake is frozen.

HERRINGBONE

This time when I saw you, you were very old,
needing my cousin's arm to keep you steady
in your herringbone jacket through the country
of the dead, where she came lately; when I
caught her eye and approached, I tried to put
my arms around you: there was nothing of you.

TRAVELS

Now that I'm old I'm the image of him,
but she couldn't see my face, even close to hers,
as she worried about her forgotten home
and where it was, the windows and the doors
all shut now, in her mind taken away
to places she had never visited,
driven by night without a reason why
to somewhere in the Free State, to get rid
of me, and coming back here in the end:
she kept trying, but memory was no use
in that last room – *Did I ever have a house?*
Her questions were scared and delirious:
Was I good? And did I have a husband?
I looked at her with his face, and I said Yes.

THE VICTIMS

We went early, but even the time has gone
where we sank into the hills, and left them like new
as the whole country freshened in the rain:
we have gone to thousands of places now.

CENTENARY 1921—2021

'There is a relation between the hours of our life and the centuries of time.'
R. W. Emerson, 'History'

1.

Six counties in the end, and a stretch at that.
You and the new country are of an age,
for you arrive on the eve of its first election
in Belfast, with two Scots who have left Scotland
for mother and father; as he stoops over
your swaddled body, Duncan McDonald
is the name he has, but was never given.
He calls you Duncan too, and everything
is ready to start afresh, to begin from here.
Your first day on this earth is a landslide.

2.

By the time you are ten, he has already
left Claremont Street: he sends you comical
postcards on your birthday, from no address,
while you grow up between two thoroughfares
that lead out of Belfast and into it,
in Craig's wee country, where next year the Prince
of Wales will open a whited sepulchre
at Stormont, laid out somewhere on the hills.
You march each weekday to Fane Street and back;
on Sundays, round the corner to Fountainville.

3.

Because you took first place in the exam
you could choose London from the G.P.O.,
posting home every week a free parcel
of laundry, while its shelters on night shifts
keep you safe; on one night off, your bedroom
falls down around you, and you sleep through it.
On Easter Tuesday in Belfast the Luftwaffe
kill nine hundred, but University Street
stands up intact; your old room waits for you
to avoid near misses, and take your uncle's pay.

4.

It was never really meant to last this long,
you still working to Jack for next to nothing,
but maybe he'll make good his promises
one day, and the whole business will be yours:
a future in saddlery. So you go up and down
the roads and small fields of Sir Basil Brooke
into the years to come: the country's young,
or as young as you are now; even the skies'
grey is a blue-grey, and these weeks and months
pass on as if they still had all to give.

5.

You buried him from your own flat in Mount Charles
with the name he had chosen: for ten years
he'd been living unknown up the Antrim Road.
You're married, with a baby on the way
who'll live in Belfast with your name, your father's.
For twenty-odd years, that pocket Emerson
has travelled with you: *Is the parent better
than the child?* You know, and you'll never say
he was illegitimate; he left your mother,
left you: *Whence, then, this worship of the past?*

6.

The sky-blue Mini is at least half rust
and has to go, though there's nothing to replace it:
buses can take you to Eliza Street
and back, to the offices at Inglis's
with their smell of bread. None of it can last,
but fifty years is a long time: O'Neill
must go, then Faulkner must go, but you
have to work anyway, and the bombs start
everywhere, every day. The once you climbed
freely into the box, the box locked.

7.

In a peaked cap and white coat, wielding the long
lollipop-stick mornings and afternoons
you shepherd hundreds of hurrying children
across the Malone and the Stranmillis Roads
in all weathers, then it's ten minutes' walk
back to your house in Dunluce Avenue:
at sixty, this is all the work you have
while everything's on hold, while the traffic-jams
wait for something to give, and you go on
for however long we all go on like this.

8.

The Boys' Brigade of nineteen-thirty-seven
is two-thirds dead, so put the photo away:
you're only looking for the dozen faces
that aren't there any more. If you go to town
the same streets aren't the same, you're not the same.
It's nobody's country now: there's just the news
you watch like a religion, unavailing
where nothing is properly the thing it was,
if it was ever that. What can you know?
You buy your last overcoat like a uniform.

9.

From this side of the ugly new hospital,
solid, catching the sun, you look straight down
on Claremont Street and University Road,
on half the town, and the country behind it
at invisible peace: Trimble and Paisley
come and go, as everything comes and goes
where people live; and that is history,
the hours of our life and the centuries
of time in the city of Belfast even:
the angularity, the shining ether.

10.

That name was never right, and it couldn't be:
illegitimate, but the real thing too,
almost as if you might be both at once.
A century of this; a century
of University Street, Botanic Avenue,
the Lisburn Road, Camden Street, crammed with ghosts
waiting, or maybe not waiting at all,
for the name they know won't last that long, and you
have been a ghost these twenty years, away
at the edge of whatever has outlived its time.

PONTOON

for Louisa

The cheetah-balloon landed who knows where.
I coax it back through time and the atmosphere
for you to catch between forefinger
and thumb, on a bald and blustery afternoon.

Count its spots until you get to twenty-one,
where you run in the late autumn over sand
that keeps your steps, as if it might hold on
to them like the perfect hand, forever.

PARAPHRASES ON PSALM 98

*O sing unto the Lord a new song: for he hath done marvellous
things.*

Not one thing that can take the place
   of another thing: remember that,
   chew/suck on that,
take notice, hold your peace,

chew it like endless bubble-gum,
suck it like a big boiled sweet:

whatever comes from you has to come
   new every time
and new is natural to him,

a billion billion facets of the earth
   new and unrepeatable
in his hand like the works of his hand,
   like grains of sand

but his palm never gets full:
   a place of safety, a space
   without need of alarm
at *death, that dark spirit, in's nervy arm.*

With his own right hand, and with his holy arm: hath he gotten himself the victory.

My dad would stretch his arm out, palm
the gobstopper I'd just unwrapped:
you could choke on that he snapped,
and it wasn't like him.
Maybe something had happened long ago,
something had happened to someone he knew,
but I never found out. I can see his hand
now: it's both strong and delicate,
the second finger raised, barely inclined
to touch the things held in it.

The Lord hath declared his salvation: his righteousness hath he openly shewed in the sight of the heathen.

A penny sheet of bubble-gum
pink, with a layer of sweet dust,
was dangerous to swallow.
Now it is bright as new.

I'm watching the sunset over Shandon Park:
orange and pale reds against the dark
at the edges of the earth. Let trouble come.

Shew yourselves joyful unto the Lord, all ye lands sing, rejoice, and
give thanks.
With trumpets also and shawms: O show yourselves joyful before
the Lord the King.

Band after band, and the noise is
    almost visible in waves
of pain: though I press my ears as

they go past, it's no good, and I whine
    and finally scream
to be taken away, taken home,

away from the skull-splitting music
    when fifes cut the air like knives,
with the Lambegs like some factory machine

slamming its rivets in, and the massed hum
    and wheeze of sickly accordions
as they carry the melody of a hymn.

Let the sea make a noise, and all that therein is: the round world,
and they that dwell therein.
Let the floods clap their hands, and let the hills be joyful together
before the Lord: for he cometh to judge the earth.

The sea is also the terror of the sea:
the sound the water makes is a dead sound
that comes to life, that you can hear inland,
that is locked somewhere within the mountains even
and waits to emerge, to split rocks and take the ground with it
into a world transfigured to sheer noise
where water judges the dry land without end.

With righteousness shall he judge the world: and the people with
equity.

Upright women and men
as they would reckon
themselves, and on firm ground

    so the evil done
    is not evil
    or else not done:
    it's all clever, civil

and foul, answering to no one,
assuming there is nobody around
and only the victim can be liable.

There is a layer of dirt in the soul
you can't see, though it can be seen;
none of us goes at our own reckoning:
we shall pay in full; we shall be paid in full.

RECKONING

Now every word I've ever said
is boxed up into emptiness,
the memories count more, and less:
is it sixty years, or twenty-odd?

GREEN GOGGLES

for Edna Longley

Turn after turn on the same long gravel walk,
and that voice going the whole time, coming
and going where he comes and goes: next week
the American listener will himself have gone
while here the sound, part song and part bee-hum,
will happen much as it has always done.
Three sonnets in a row spoken by heart
with not a single line yet written down:
what do you say to that? What will he say,
if anything? Nowadays, his eyes hurt
and he wears green goggles in the open air,
old and alarming. Harmlessly
the gravel crimp-crumps, and it's hard to hear
those half-sung words, or remember what they were.

They part with courtesies, a young widower
striding apart from grief, and the famous man
who could tell him nothing new, as it turned out.
The sad vacationer hasn't – he hasn't yet –
written a paragraph to last: he'll go back
and write up all of this, write down that voice
with marks in gravel for its only trace;
not once in two hours did he see those eyes.
An ocean and a continent away
genius and youth will do their vanishing trick,
with rows of aphorisms like armour plate.
To a man in his twenties, a man of sixty-three
is an old man, never to be improved:
life is the living, not the having lived.

AUTOGRAPHS

Heather and Lesley, Roisin, Hilary:
names in the coloured ink all seem to bleed
with decades of rain into that blotchy sky.
Lesley was a grandmother when she died.

DEPARTURES

i.m. Christopher Butler

I

They take off at no special time of day,
and travel where they never come back from;
the red earth that is brittle and long dry
takes them in, even as it forgets them.

II

Music and books and movies and all the rest
of what you loved and what you made astounding
are not the same, now that it's time I left
this place where you could always leave me standing.

III

Thirty-four cartons that I've filled, and half
as many again for the skip, unplaced
for good, with emptiness on every shelf
and nobody inside that room: all waste.

IV

The dark above downturned faces is a cowl.
Three men are standing over a bowl of fire:
stagey, but much like any ritual
when nobody knows what the ritual is for.

V

A big box plastered with stickers and straps,
its origin and destination not the same,
or probably not: words peel away in strips
on the poem where I'm posting myself home.

THEN

It is either bedtime or getting-up time:
light from a storm drills the soil into grooves,
and this could be a nightmare or a good dream.
Victorian children sit up in their graves.

ROXBURY GOTHIC 1832

Even in her pretty miniature
something about the face
is pained, tubercular;
his bride of a year,
bride of the minister
who now can believe no more.

Cold Boston nights, the fire
not tended and going out,
when he will just stare
at the wall, seeing nothing there
into each desolate morning.
God or whosoever
(such is His greatness)
plainly cannot care,
and a whole year goes over
only to start again.
From frost nights to spring nights
and smothering summer,
it is all the one night-time
for her dumbstruck widower.

She said she was going ahead
to wait for him: but where?
Wait in that damp brick vault
or behind the evening star?
There is too much hurt to bear
and even this long after,
the big wound won't heal.

To cauterize his grief
he has to go and see her,
open the narrow box
and somehow look in her face:
the heart that he will tear
in two is his own heart.
She has gone on before
and yet, yes, she is nowhere,
with a sad girl's face
not her face any more.

A PRIDE OF THE SPIRIT

A butterfly that came too early in March
took twenty minutes of the beating sun.
I wanted you to join me then and watch,
but I was too late, and you were too soon.

SELF-RELIANCE

Hard snow was pitiless, and white as death:
breathe it in and you would breathe death itself,
while the soul escaped at your mouth and nostrils
with nowhere to go, until it disappeared.

You couldn't know you grew up in a prison
until you saw that those were bars; you thought
your way out, and just the thinking was strong:
everything was strong, each thing a first thing.

Between a snow-drift and the sky, only
the tallest places lifted their heads; trees
had bent deep and awry, not strong enough;
one dark spire was lost in the wilderness.

ARRIVAL

This must be where I was going to all
those years: the truth is that I never knew,
and nobody appears to help me tell
the shape of it, tell above from below.

ESCAPE

for Angela Leighton

Liking the shape it makes, I want to take
that box out of itself, call it a form,
a volume held within a solid frame
where the sides open and close like a book.
If there's movement inside, it doesn't show,
and anyway the planks are windowpanes,
so I can see all I already knew
was there: stillness is stillness of the lines
that move in their own way, that taper in
if you watch carefully, and if you listen.
It's not just that there's nobody inside,
but that whoever was in there has gone
– look, gone – and you can feel where they have been.

But inside, everything is far away,
the air, and sounds, the day and night even,
so you have to make them: narrow escapes
are pre-planned in a voice speaking, where steps
pace evenly, or shuffle across a poem
to click, echo and patter in a tap-dance
or tread the worn path to a burial-place,
crunching the frost or slipping across ice
without deception, with no reason why,
only to do the same thing over again.
All a poet can do today is warn,
but maybe not today: let's wait and see.

As he went into his outsized milk-churn,
the once-Hungarian Harry Houdini
wound his limbs about one enormous chain
when the lid was bolted down – did he come
out to the cheers each time as the same man?
Even in full view, nobody could see him.
Ehrich was Ehri, and Ehri was Harry,
then Harry was out of there for twenty-
odd years at the very top, leaving the box
empty each time, and not behind their backs
but before their eyes.
                Whoever listens
hard enough might hear what is going on:
either it's broad day or the stroke of midnight –
inside containers, the two are the same,
and maybe no time is the right time to get out;
nevertheless, you have to get out on time
to fill the space; as now my Canadian
beech-bowl is filled with Sicilian lemons.

INCIDENT

A crowd half-gathers: people leave and join,
and nobody speaks much. Men look at things.

*

Boxes lie open and empty; some are full
of nothing much, some soak the shadows up
unnoticed at the edges of it all,
whatever it is – it may not be anything.

*

Bottles and bright-coloured wrappers in a heap
just left there – why? – and nobody belongs:
sometimes the same ones go and come back again.

*

The inside of one box is made of light.

*

As many leaving now as happening by:
some of them look like me when I was young,
but no, they've gone; it's all jumbled away,
throughother, and long night-time hides the lot.

DISTANCE

I've driven in one direction now for years,
with nothing on the clock that can tell me
the distance put between my life and yours:
this is as far away as I can be.

CONCORD

for Karen O'Brien

I have forgotten most of what I've read:
but that summer it was *The Blithedale Romance*,
of which I recall only philosophers
and snow, and maybe wrongly. On the road
from Cambridge most weekends we would chance
on anywhere within a day's reach of us –
one year married, and you still twenty-odd:
both of us far from home, glad to be there,
we saw more than it's easy to remember.
That was midsummer, not the fall, and not
hard winter, those two seasons that transcend
the truth as I flick back through pages to find
evidence for what cannot have been the case.
Maybe it wasn't us, maybe the spot
was somewhere else, for everything's misplaced
from books to life, then back to a book again
where it can stay, unsociable, unseen.
Our love-stories had no twists in the plot
or really any plot at all – just this
drifting together with no consequence

as we walked in Concord, and I went to see
if I could find bean-rows at Walden Pond,
though by now the market-garden geography
had gone, and that defiant solitude
had gone where we followed the tourist-trail
that wound back over itself, although all
it could remind us of had been
forgotten long since. We were hand in hand
when we chose to leave that statelet of innocence,

and slipped away past Emerson's old manse
on a day that was nearly unmemorable.
We let the town put us into the distance –
much further now, where in the end I'm lost
in self-reliance, with less I can understand,
then less and less, whichever year it was
or is, whatever seasons I confuse,
coating those sidewalks with impossible frost.

*When Israel went out of Egypt, the house of Jacob from a people of
strange language;*

For weeks on end, it was hotter
inside than out: that was the way.

The land was enormous, and not yours;
one day was much like another day.

There was nothing to be done, until
it was done, and nothing to say:

you could talk to them, they gave you jobs
to do; you weren't obliged to obey.

But their very tongue was a prison
whose every word would make you stay

when really there was no point in talking.
Sometimes you have to walk away.

Judah was his sanctuary, and Israel his dominion.

What little land there is
                  that I can call my own
has just a house on it
                  and a scrap of weedy garden;
the land of my sanctuary
                  is not much more than a beach,
long and empty, some
                  cliffs and a mile or two
of cliff-walks, a stretch
                  of sky across the sea;
rock-pools with peculiar
                  small fish, and flora
not seen elsewhere, the tiny
                  clenched blooms of white
and red, sudden lavish
                  toadstools that open up
polka-dot canopies, while in
                  some protected ground
the actual toads are boggling
                  at extinction's edge.
My people are no more than
                  a family, and I walk them
into this nameless land
                  I name the land of refuge.

The sea saw it and fled: Jordan was driven back

The light was blue and pale green, beating
as waves pushed up to and over
bare chalk, that from the cave was
an oval window on the sea.

Standing there, you felt after a while
it must have been the rocks moving
upwards away, and the sea falling
that you watched from that damp tunnel.

Above, the path led to a border
you couldn't cross, and the midday
sun flashed on signs to Rosh Hanikra,
the inland and coast-roads of Israel.

What ailed thee, O thou sea, that thou fleddest? thou Jordan, that thou wast driven back?
Ye mountains, that ye skipped like rams; and ye little hills, like lambs?

If you only see time from where you are in it
then solid ground, like the hills and the mountains,
never moves; but time is not just where you are,
and the rocks and all the waters of the world
change places, dance around each other, jump
into and out of patterns, endlessly: they
seem slow only because you're going so fast
over the earth that you can barely register.

Rivers draw back and change their courses, vast
mountain ranges, stacked up and up and up
where nobody sets foot, and the walkable
low hills, their sides covered in livestock,
leap together with the directionless energy
of lambs in the springtime in an open field.

Tremble, thou earth, at the presence of the Lord, at the presence of the God of Jacob;

And sometimes, yes, you have to walk.
As I'm standing here, I must block

sunshine as it flattens the air,
but going on my way I clear

more space: there is a shadow still
distinct from me for a short while,

yet as I grow smaller the ground
is land that clouds and sun have gained,

brighter and further, until all
you see is one glow of detail,

bearing that last speck of me late
away. Now I am only light.

Which turned the rock into a standing water, the flint into a fountain of waters.

The house of Jacob and the God of Jacob:
not words in air, but a promise.

A puddle of fresh water on the rock:
not rain, but a miracle.

The way people are drawn to fountains:
not air, but water held in the air.

MAJORITY

I can remember turning twenty-one;
I spent the night with a sentimental novel
about Ireland, the death of innocence,
death: really it was never all that good,

and nobody would read it now. I cried,
but I think that was the whiskey. No one
knew, and maybe it was just a moment:
I hardly knew myself, and still don't know.

THE PILLOW

I turn and talk to you before I sleep,
talk to you in my head, for you're not here;
but you listen, and you smile, until you slip
from the pillow into all that came before.

ANABASIS

for Catriona Graffius

A book of verse at the age of twenty-four
might have been the last, for there was no room
for poetry in the Quai d'Orsay, or for
Alexis St. Léger in poems when they came
long after that, at work in China. *St.-*
John Perse had the ring of untruth, just
distinct enough: *Anabase*, the voyage up
that you choose to take, or take if you must
as a responsible, important man,
when the one imperative is to be in the room,
to be going there, and never to stop
until things stop you.

                    That happens. Now
an ex-poet is helping Daladier
at Munich, trying hard to keep at bay
Italy and Germany by giving just
enough and no more – there's a photograph.
Any room, though, is never room enough:
while Chamberlain has the memo in his hand
and Mussolini's eyes dart out of the way,
Hitler stares down the camera to the end;
St.-John Perse daydreams of Guadeloupe.

Is it backwards or upwards, the journey
from now to twenty-four? If I tell you
how much I want to turn around and see
that age again, it may be only as true
as the scrap of paper that it's written on.
In Marie-Galente, where they make black rum
that burns, those twenty-odd years would be old
enough: how many are in the little room?
Has something been agreed? Will we be told?
The world is an everywhere, but so is time:
St.-John Perse will marry at seventy-one.

READER

She tires of my book, and puts it to one side.
The sky's reflections are reflected where
she looks a long time in her lover's eyes
and sees herself. That day, they read no more.

HISTORY

Midnight was all clouds, and then breaking clouds
when the moon came out, a moon full and risen:
what I was seeing made me an archangel
at the creation of light and of the world.

And from then on the past never existed
apart from me, small creatures under leaves
were me as well, and moonlit flying insects
proved over again the transmigration of souls,

for men and women are only one half human:
the other half is everywhere, and now
is all there has been ever, when I know
just how the Sphinx must solve her own riddle.

SPECIMENS

Remember a dead butterfly in the light,
and its dry, peeling wings you couldn't fix?
This is the real thing, and it is too late:
my caterpillar squirming in a matchbox.

PITHOS

for A.E. Stallings

Whatever is inside it doesn't matter:
in a way, what's outside is what keeps the shape.
We have both been close to this man-made jar
in our time, as we tried to measure up
to it, to take its measure, years apart
on the same spot. Now neither of us is there,
but we're able to describe it in the air,
using our hands for what words can't report,
just the size, the curves, the containment of it,
an ancient thing that everything comes from,
as tall as we are, rounded out and down,
an empty vessel that can fill the room,
a jar, a *pithos*, nothing so angular
as a box – it must have been here forever,
shaping a volume that nothing will capture.

The lid is off; the lid was never found:
maybe it was lost somewhere in good time,
or else it's in the soil of a Greek island.
What we have anyway is the whole form,
open at the top. Now it is long ago
I realized the sounds of my own name
were quantities that wouldn't fit in a poem,
but I wonder when it was that you first knew
Alicia Stallings ends a hexameter
or heard that, or saw it written in stone?
The sound of a poem is a poem's measure.
Michael Longley (two trochees) used the flat
of his hand in the air to describe an *S*
for the shape that a good lyric might take on

(across from him, I saw it in reverse),
tenderly stroking the sheer emptiness
and saying how all the poems in a book
of poems make a line that's like an arc,
where every cadence measures a caress.

Some words you can't translate: you have to make
them up and make them do – and that word, hope,
elpis, left clinging under the jar's lip,
might be the thing on sufferance, if you like,
but leave it; and sorrow, that goes about
dry land and oceans, really doesn't need
much help, yet it's an element to ride,
to make shapes over and against: what's said
is done, is what we have and what we lack.
Open a poem, and everything pours out.

DELIVERY

I send myself like a parcel on a world tour,
as if I would ever see places again,
or as if there were places for me to enter
in a box that nobody can open.

SALT

Paraphrase on St.-John Perse, Anabase I

You stagger out of a bad dream, wounded,
your head on my shoulder and your face to me.
I don't know when this was, or when it will be
in that desert of salt: we are surrounded.

*

Water is running somewhere from its den
far inland, over grey sands where the sea
yawns behind everything, in eternity:
strike camp, then, with the frail breezes at dawn.

*

I don't know where we start from, or how long
we're travelling: the sun under eclipse
is still the sun; there is salt on my lips
that touch yours as the dry winds thump and sing.

*

You watch thorn bushes crumpling to fire
and heat that blurs and wobbles over the flames;
whoever speaks these things gives them their names:
mineral blocks, icebergs on a parched shore.

*

My soul is pure as water full of sand;
following trade-routes, it is ready to do
business, wasted with thirst, dreaming for you
weapons of morning, bright spears in the ground.

TEARS OF THE MUSES

for Alice Goodman

They should probably form some kind of a ring,
don't you think? They're moving in step together,
and we half-hear whatever they are singing
as if we each had only the one good ear,
and that turned away. Of course, all the other
noises just carry on with the crash and blare,
with their buzz and fizz, their shrilling and pinging
in some dimension beyond any sense:
yet that, too, is a thing to be made sense of.
Between the music and the noise, the dance
and the clumsiness of bodies falling down
across each other, an over and above
picture from the imagination-drone
proves everything's all right.
                              If you look there,
there he is, trigged out in his courting gear
on one side of the Muses' dancehall, shy
as a flushed teenager or the class dunce,
but ready to give it a go, and ask.
Between the gorgon and the basilisk,
something has turned to stone, and awkwardly
he makes a play for poor Andromeda
(or some such name) until you catch his eye
and there, behind the poker face, he's daring
you to laugh: *martyr to musophilia*
recited like a grim comic ground-bass
beneath that florid music, more or less,
like one half of a joke in the routine –

on his baseball cap it says *Musophilus*,
so that's us told. The dance starts up again,

and it's all come and go, a sort of line-dance,
a take your partners for the do-si-do
to scrambling fiddles and a washboard, then
blitzed zombies trying to put on a show
with drums and snatches of deafening, virtuosic
guitar that's strangling itself in feedback.
Babel comes though as *tinnitus*, within
that sound the notes of an old chapel hymn,
so back we go now to a metrical psalm.
But look, look twice, for all of them are crying
where they move together, choking on the song,
mouthing its words that must be beautiful
if you're close up; and there he is, held in
near to the circle, tripping without a fall,
his arms stretched out and their arms holding him.

REFLECTING BOX

The space is broken, or there is no space
deep in the surface where you see my mark
catching the light: will you be in that place
to hold me if I waken in the dark?

RONNIE

It was above the shop, but open
       so you could sit at one
of the work-tables and look down
at the whole showroom beneath you
       where furniture from a dozen
living-rooms seemed to have been arranged
to face all the daylight coming through
from the Cregagh Road, where it rained
and shone over one wall of glass:
       that's where the workshop was,
with its big rounds of carpet and underlay
up to the roof, tool-boxes put by
or open, tape-measures, guillotines
       to cut in straight lines,
       canisters, pots of glue,
       a board with dates and addresses,
then ledgers that had sizes and shapes in
against the lengths of rolls, a whole
       upstairs den you would hardly
notice from down among the chairs
and armchairs, sofas and deep-pile
rugs in the shop itself.

              It was here
that Ronnie would work, or get ready
to work when he'd go out to fit
       square miles of carpet
like lightning, and exactly every time,
so well had it been planned and cut,
       in room after room after room
       everywhere, all over Belfast:
       I used to sit with him

while I fiddled with some Airfix kit
and he zipped ahead, precise and fast,
            ready to load up and get on.
I thought that I was breathing in
purpose and skill from being half-hidden
with a good view of everything below,
            and loved that air of know-how,
though really I didn't have a clue
about what I knew how to do.

            It was fifty years ago,
more, and before long I was gone,
Ronnie was gone, and Milligan's
was gone too with its furniture
            and carpets sent to nowhere,
and the office downstairs on the left
where my mother kept the books was gone,
while the place to watch from, make things in
            went inside, or sank down
            inside me like a lead weight,
            like ballast to keep me straight
but slow, as I worked and worried out of sight,
hutched in the dark, with light from one side
            to cover what was made;
unlike Ronnie, so sharp and so smart
he could finish two houses in one day.

            Those new carpets and underlay
will have got old, will have been thrown away,
            but now in the lighted dark
I can smell them, I can breathe in work
and readiness and quiet: it is all
            as still as still.

A PRESUMPTION OF THE MIND

Or say that I'm the man shut in a box,
breathing and turning and not knowing why.
These night-waters are walls of falling bricks.
The sea is close. The sea is far away.

THE FACE

That whole last year there was nothing of her,
and whenever you hugged her you hugged bones,
death inching over where the life had been
so steadily you'd be crying as you left.
I couldn't come and hold her hands as they wasted,
sending a letter instead to Killyleagh
for my cousin to hear read out: *she cried sore*
you said, as she went into her children's arms,
away to the hotels and the country ballrooms
and the showbands playing half the night
far out of town, dresses, hairdos, good looks,
men in cheap suits and Brylcreem at the bar,
seaside trinkets, songs about broken hearts,
and the last face you saw: *sure it would fear ye.*

THE KNOT

Like the just-snapped grass, and like a grass-blade
that's strong enough to be looped, pulled and bent,
then somehow hold itself tight in its own lifeblood:
love that is unavailing, unrelenting.

OMAHA

for Fran Brearton

We were pushing on across rainy dunes
to face the sea on that cold summer day
when we saw coming in through skirr and spray
first the head and shoulders, then all at once
an entire swimmer, wading out towards us
past rocks there at the mouth of a little cave
where high tide was at its least dangerous,
up to firm sand, with us two just above.

I had been showing you the tussocky edge
of a golf course that wasn't a golf course then,
more than a century ago – where, I believe,
as a gangly teenager born the wrong age
he used to lose himself out in the open
between a pale sky and Atlantic waves,
while he daydreamed of supernatural flesh
emerging from the water in one flash
of cold to come and take him.

                              Nobody
could see the boy as he was shuddering under
the pressure of the sand, and yet twenty-
odd years on, he was able to remember
every moment, walking above the beach
near a house facing out over *La Manche*,
between one woman, his lover too late,
and another, a girl too early to love.
All he would do was watch the breakers launch
and land the whole day, like the tide's heartbeat,
across a grey and white stretch of wet sand.

When he was dead, more than three decades later,
boys ran from those waves, leaving their lives behind
on Omaha, boys virgin for ever
one cold summer day at Colleville-sur-Mer.

He watched the girl as she danced, with her hair
coming down, long hair that he might wind
and unwind by taking it in a chaste hand:
she came to him first before she was born
in the other century, at a magical turn
of the tide, and in those dunes where we were.

DROP

If somebody asked, Where are you falling to?
I couldn't answer; but out of charity
some drop will open itself, some gap through
and down, where my own weight will carry me.

COMPENSATION

Even that crow, out alone where the trees are,
is part of a mechanism, in the balance
of seconds that keep the minutes and the hours
with oiled metal flywheels and coiled springs,

all to and fro and back and forth, give, take,
just to keep steady as the world globes itself
in a drop of dew, look, and your friends are gone
to nowhere, for the earth is a makeweight

where angels must give place to archangels.
Fear is the carrion crow: he has seen
something in us, even from far away,
so he waits; we cannot let our angels go.

AT BELFAST LOUGH

There are five oystercatchers working the low tide
where I've walked at the speed my dad would walk
this half an hour; now that his face is mine
he's back, I suppose, and the birds must see him
on the grey beach in a hat and overcoat:
he's at a loss for words, too long awake,
and a hundred years old, or as old as I am.
Lough-water here feels smaller than the land
and sky, than the clouds that are all round,
or the working city it has come to meet.
There's nobody to watch us on the sand
except for that one departing aeroplane
far above us, far above us in the rain
while all the time the waves break, break.
There's only this. There's nothing time can mend.

by Emerson, and poems 5 and 9 of 'Centenary' quote from Emerson's 'History': 'Is the parent better than the child into whom he has cast his ripened being? Whence, then, this worship of the past?'; 'Time dissipates to shining ether the solid angularity of facts'. (All of these sources are in a pocket-sized book, *Emerson's Essays: A Selection* ed. C.L. Hind (1906), my father's battered copy of which is inscribed with the date 1938.) The poem 'Green Goggles' (p.36) makes use of an anecdote (about Wordsworth) in Emerson's *English Traits* (1856), 'First Visit to England'; 'Roxbury Gothic 1832' (p.41) stems from a journal entry by Emerson relating to his deceased first wife, Ellen Louisa Tucker (1811–1831).

'Paraphrases on Psalm 98' (p.29) and 'Paraphrases on Psalm 114' (p.52) first appeared in my pamphlet *Five Psalms* (Agenda Editions, 2021). The translated verses from the Psalms at the head of each poem are from Miles Coverdale's Psalter of 1535.

NOTES

The book's epigraph is from *Anabase* (1924) by St.-John Perse (Alexis St. Léger Léger (1887–1975)), I *iv*: in T.S. Eliot's translation, 'and the sea at morning like a pride of the spirit' (1928), then 'and the sea at morning like a presumption of the mind' (1930). 'Solitude' (p.17) and 'Salt' (p.68) are free adaptations and extensions of passages from the same work, and the poem 'Anabasis' (p.60) revolves also around Perse's career as a diplomat and poet. I am indebted to Catriona Graffius for introducing me to Perse's poem, to Stephen Romer for helping me to approach it, and to Rosanna Warren for generously sharing her own memories of Perse and her mother, Eleanor Clark: for details of their brief relationship see Rosanna Warren, 'Foreign Affairs: The many lives and loves of the mysterious St.-John Perse', *The American Scholar* (Jan. 2023).

'Centenary 1921-2021' (p.23): My father, Duncan McDonald, was born in Belfast on 23 May, 1921; the first election to the Parliament of Northern Ireland was held on 24 May, 1921. This sequence of poems contains names of some Prime Ministers in the Northern Ireland Parliament: James Craig, Viscount Craigavon (Prime Minister, 1921-1940), Sir Basil Brooke, Viscount Brookeborough (Prime Minister, 1943–1963), Terence O'Neill (Prime Minister, 1963–1969), and Brian Faulkner (Prime Minister, 1971–1972). David Trimble was First Minister in the Northern Ireland Assembly from 1998-2001, and Ian Paisley held the same post in 2007–2008.

Several poems draw upon work by Ralph Waldo Emerson. 'Self-Reliance' (p.44), 'History' (p.63), and 'Compensation' (p.81) take their titles, as well as some phrases, from essays

GLAMOUR

No snow all winter; now in April, snow:
already blossoming, the plum tree wears
bonnets of cut glass over every flower
and all across its leaves, where the dust was.